P9-DMY-202

How an e-Book Works

by Amanda StJohn ❀ illustrated by Bob Ostrom

Wonder Books
An Imprint of The Child's World®
childsworld.com

Published by The Child's World®
800-599-READ • childsworld.com

ISBN Information
9781503865389 (Reinforced Library Binding)
9781503866225 (Portable Document Format)
9781503867062 (Online Multi-user eBook)
9781503867901 (Electronic Publication)

LCCN 2022939183

Printed in the United States of America

About the Author
Amanda StJohn is an author
and a public librarian. She is
fascinated by singing frogs
and animal tracks and enjoys
apricot tea and knitting.

About the Illustrator
Bob Ostrom has been
illustrating children's books for
more than twenty years. A
graduate of the New England
School of Art & Design at
Suffolk University, Bob has
worked for such companies
as Disney, Nickelodeon,
and Cartoon Network. He
lives in North Carolina.

When Stew Rabbit arrived at the library, he marched to the children's room. He found his best friend and smiled. His bunny teeth shined. "Hey, Opal!"

"Hey," she called back.

Stew rubbed his cheek. "What are you doing there?"

"Reading this e-book," Opal Owl answered.

"What's an e-book?" Stew asked, sitting down.

"*e-Book* means electronic book," Opal explained. "Instead of reading words on the pages of a book, we read e-books on a computer or e-reader."

"And that's an e-reader?" asked Stew.

Opal held up her **device**. "Right. I read my e-books on this."

Opal handed Stew her e-reader. He peered at it and turned it around and upside down.

"My e-reader is a WormyBook," she added.

"There are other types of e-readers, then?" Stew asked quite curiously.

"Sure!" Opal whistled. "Just like there are different types of cars to drive around in, there are different kinds of e-readers to read e-books on."

"So," Stew began, "how does an e-book work?

The First e-Book

The Declaration of Independence was first digitized in 1971. E-books really didn't gain popularity until the 2000s.

6

Opal thought for a moment. "Well, how do you usually find library books?"

"Easy! I use the library **catalog**," said Stew.

"That's exactly what I did to find this e-book," agreed Opal.

Opal led Stew over to a computer station. On the library's main website, she showed Stew the e-books catalog button. "Click this. You'll see e-books you can borrow from the library."

On the computer screen, Stew saw three lists. They said: "For Adults, For Teens, For Kids."

"Click 'For Kids'?" Stew guessed.

"Good job." Opal clicked on the list for kids. "Pick one, Stew. And if you don't see a book you like, you can always ask a librarian for help."

Stew found a book called *Sunny and Luna.* "That one!"

When Opal clicked on the book, the computer screen asked: "Which **format** do you want: PDF, EPUB, or WB?"

"What does this stuff mean?" asked Stew.

"Don't worry." Opal was cool as ever. "We want WB."

Stew raised his eyebrow. "How do you know?"

Opal answered, "WB stands for WormyBook. My e-reader takes WB formats. WormyBook's instructions told me."

Stew pointed at the other formats. "Other e-readers might read these formats?"

"Right," nodded Opal.

Books on Your Phone

Many people like to use their smartphone as an e-reader. Applications (or "apps" for short) let you read books right on your smartphone.

Opal clicked the correct format, then clicked "check out." Next, the computer screen asked for her library card number. Opal looked at her library card. She typed the number on her card into the computer. She double-checked her typing and clicked the OK button.

The computer went to a new website. Stew and Opal could see the cover of *Sunny and Luna.* The screen said, "Available to download."

"Can we read your e-book now?" asked Stew.

"Not yet," Opal shook her head. "It's not on my e-reader yet."

"Well, how does an e-book get onto your e-reader?" pressed Stew.

"We **sync** up. Like this . . . " Opal opened her bag. From a little pouch she pulled out a long white cable called a USB cord. Opal plugged one end of the cord into her WormyBook. She plugged the other end into the library computer.

"Press the WormyBook's power button," she said to Stew.

With the power on, the WormyBook connected to the computer.

"So what do we do next?" asked Stew.

"We follow the instructions on the screen," replied Opal. "If you have a different e-reader, the steps to download a book might be different. If you get stuck, a librarian can help you."

So what do we do next?

11

"So what do we have to do for *your* e-reader?" asked Stew.

"I'll show you," replied Opal. She pointed to the screen. "See the **icon** for my WormyBook? It appeared on the computer desktop when I plugged in my device."

She clicked on the *Sunny and Luna* link and its icon appeared on the computer desktop too. She dragged the book icon on top of the WormyBook icon. The computer screen said, "Download complete."

Next, they needed to eject their e-reader from the computer. This would end the sync and make sure the e-book was saved correctly. Opal clicked "Eject."

"You may now remove your device safely," the computer screen said.

Opal rolled up her USB cord. "I'd better put this away before I lose it."

Stew and Opal left the computer station so someone else could use it. They plopped onto a giant beanbag. On her WormyBook, Opal went to the main screen.

There, on the digital bookshelf, sat a copy of *Sunny and Luna.* Other e-books sat on Opal's bookshelf too. She had *Wind in the Willows,* a story about a toad and a frog. There was even an e-book on how to bake cookies.

Opal's cookbook had a banner that said "2 days."

"What does that mean?" asked Stew.

"The cookbook is a library e-book," she explained.

"So, you have to return the book to the library in two days?" asked Stew.

"Kind of," Opal tilted her head. "Actually, you never have to return e-books."

Stew was puzzled. "Then . . . why does it say two days?"

"Because," began Opal, "in two days, the e-book will disappear!"

"Nuh-uh. That's not true." Stew was sure Opal was teasing.

"It's totally true!" she squealed. "It goes *poof*!"

Stew thought about what happened when he returned a library book late. He had to pay money for a **fine**. "You don't have to pay any fines for e-books?"

"Never," declared Opal. "Because the book returns itself. Cool, huh?"

Doing Away with Library Fines

Some libraries are considering ending fines for books that are overdue. The idea is to help make sure the library is always a welcoming place.

"How else is borrowing e-books different from borrowing books?" asked Stew.

"That sounds like a question for Ms. Mantis," said Opal.

Off they went to find Ms. Mantis, the children's librarian. Ms. Mantis was decorating the bulletin board with cutout clowns.

"Hi, Ms. Mantis," Stew said, clearing his throat.

Opal asked, "How is borrowing e-books different than borrowing books?"

"I like your question!" Ms. Mantis smiled. "Tell me, how many books can you take home at once?"

"Ten," answered Opal firmly.

"Well, you can have only two e-books at one time," said the librarian.

Learning this gave Stew a new thought.

"Ms. Mantis?" Stew stroked a whisker. "I return my books right after reading them. Can I return e-books early too?"

19

"Sure," sang Ms. Mantis. "Plug in your WormyBook. I'll show you how."

Opal synced her device with the computer.

"See that little arrow by your book?" Ms. Mantis paused. "Click it once."

The arrow showed some options. One said, "Return this book to the library."

"Wow," said Opal. "I didn't know about that."

Just to practice, Opal clicked the arrow by her cookbook. She clicked "Return this book" and the book disappeared—*poof*!

"Whoa," Stew gasped. "You weren't kidding, Opal. When a book goes *poof*!, it disappears for good!"

Tips to Remember

✓ To check out library e-books, you need a library card.

✓ Don't share your library card with anyone.

✓ Use the advanced search feature to find only the e-books written in your e-reader's preferred format.

✓ Don't unplug your device until you eject it on the computer screen. This will make sure your files are saved correctly.

✓ Ask your librarian for help when you need it.

Glossary

catalog (KAT-uh-log): A catalog is the complete list of items a library has to offer. Stew and Opal searched the catalog for e-books to read.

device (dih-VISE): A device is a piece of technology used for a specific purpose, like reading e-books. Opal used an e-reader device to read e-books.

fine (FINE): A fine is money you might have to pay if you damage or lose a library book or return it late. Stew will have to pay a fine if he doesn't return his library books on time.

format (FOR-mat): A format is the way a digital file, such as an e-book, is saved on the computer. Opal's e-books were in the format used for WormyBook e-readers.

icon (EYE-kahn): An icon is a picture image that represents an e-book, e-reader device, or other item on a computer. Opal saw the WormyBook icon on her computer desktop.

sync (SINGK): Sync comes from the word *synchronize*, meaning to get two things to work together. Opal had to sync her e-reader with the library computer.

Wonder More

1. Have you ever read an e-book? Did you use an e-reader or a smartphone?

2. What are three new things you learned about e-books from this book?

3. Library catalogs were not always kept on computers. They used to be kept on paper. Which type do you think is easier to use? Explain your answer.

4. Some people prefer to read paper books instead of e-books. Which way do you like to read books? Explain your answer.

Find Out More

In the Library

Dean, James. *Pete the Cat Checks Out the Library.*
New York, NY: HarperCollins, 2018.

StJohn, Amanda. *How a Library Works.* Parker, CO: The Child's World, 2023.

Taylor, Chloe. *The Big Book of Invisible Technology: A Look at How Things Work for Kids.* Rockridge Press: Emeryville, CA: 2020.

On the Web

Visit our website for links about library skills: **childsworld.com/links**

Note to Parents, Caregivers, Teachers, and Librarians: We routinely verify our Web links to make sure they are safe and active sites. So encourage your readers to check them out!

Index

borrowing, 7, 10, 17, 18
catalog, 7
Declaration of Independence, 4
downloading, 10-11, 13
e-readers, 4, 8, 11, 13, 21
fines, 17

formats, 8, 10, 21
icons, 13
library card, 10, 21
returning, 17, 18, 21
smartphones, 8
syncing, 11, 13, 21